THIS NOTEBOOK BELONGS TO:

____

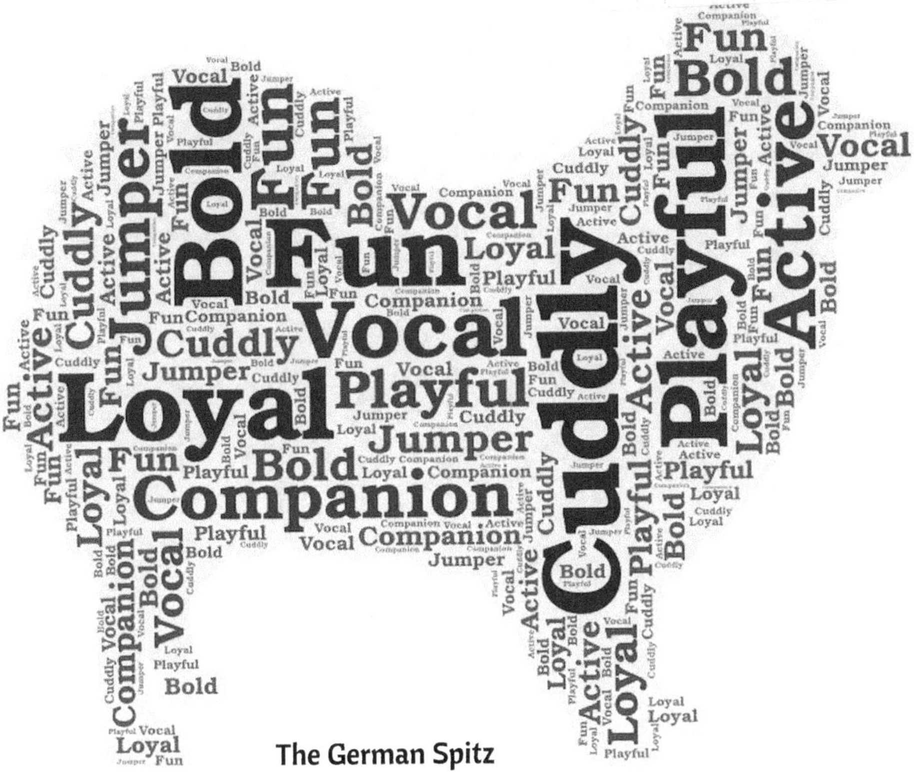

The German Spitz

SPITZ NOTES German Spitz edition
A Dogspiration Publication

Cover model: Teddy

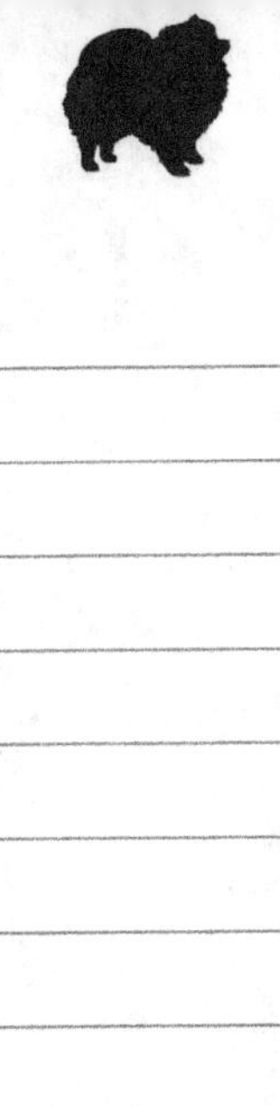

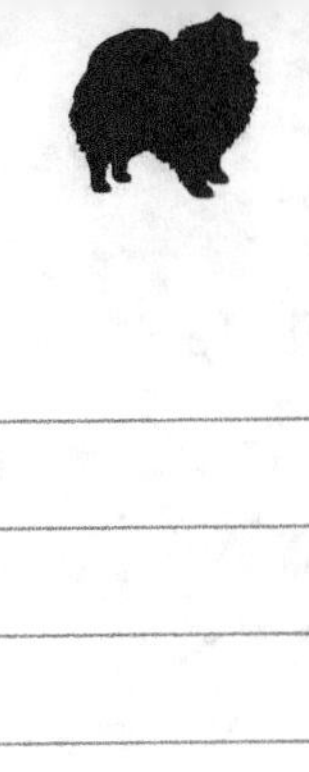

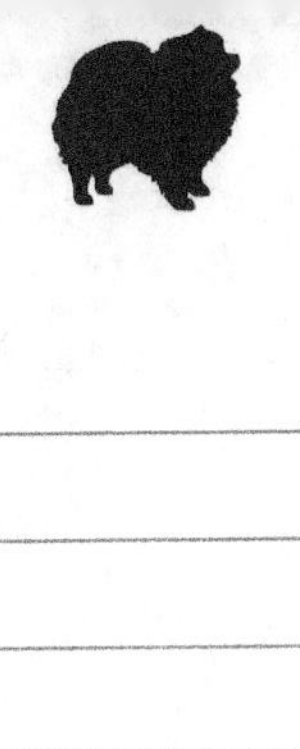

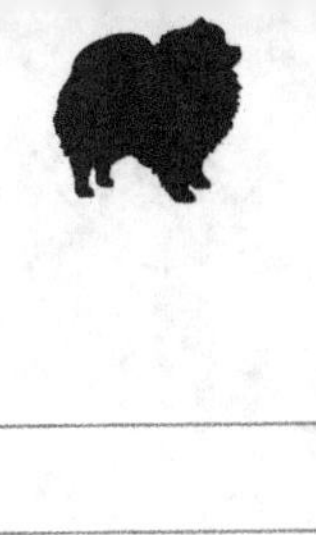

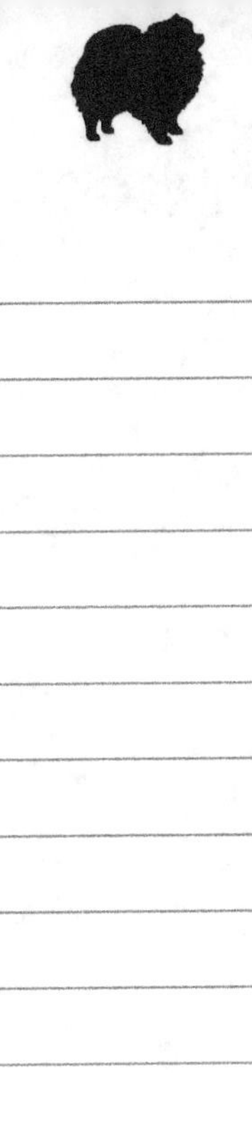

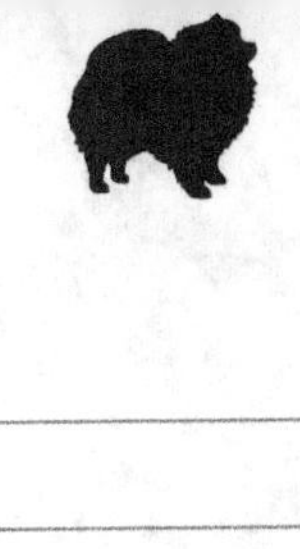

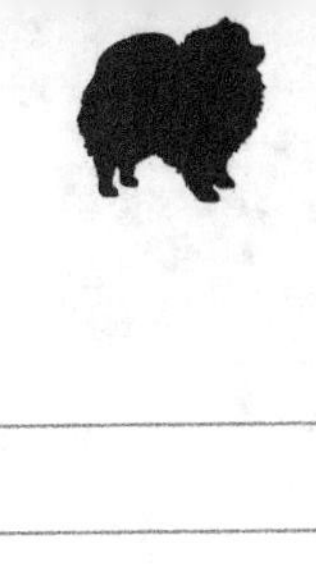

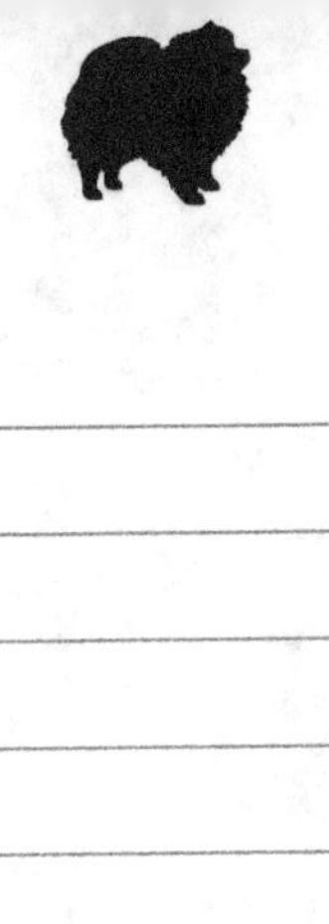

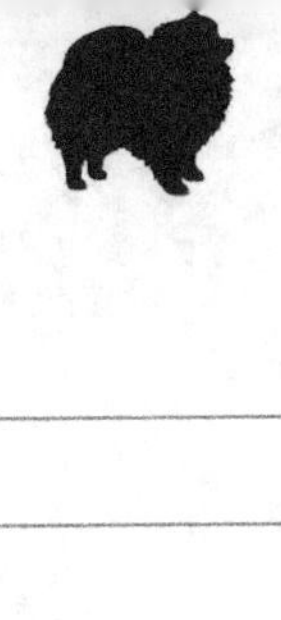

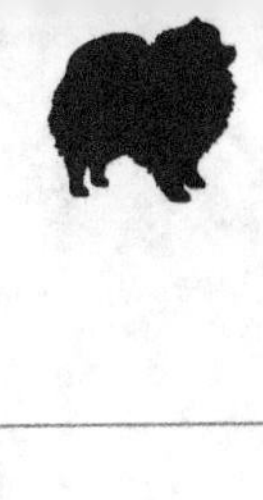

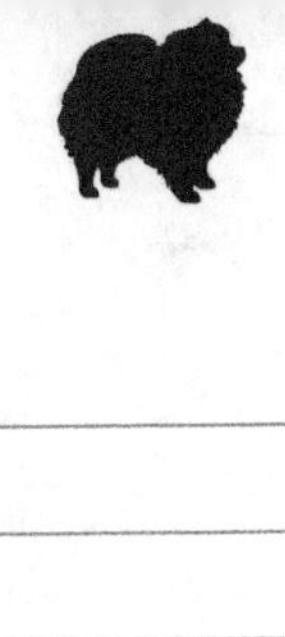

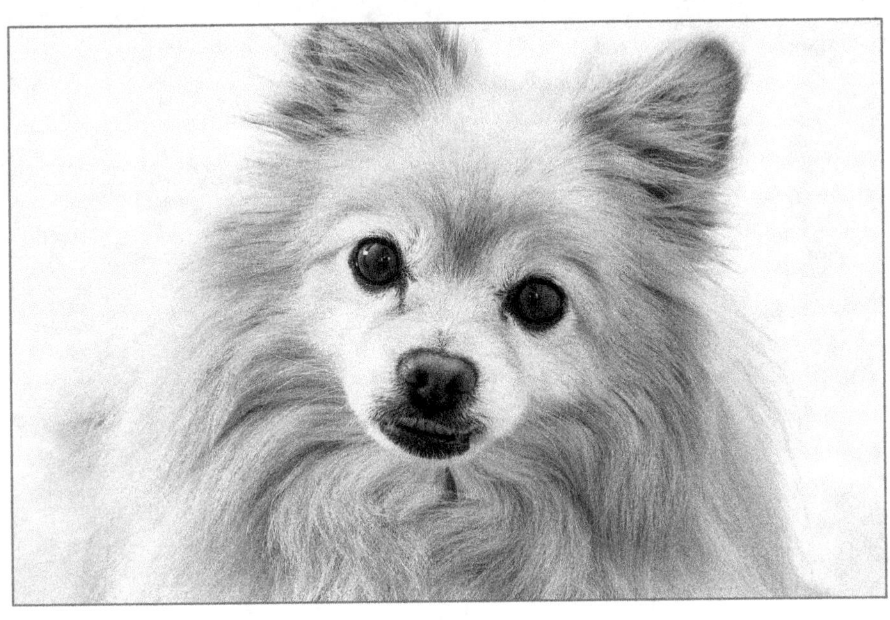